Contents

Revised Edition

STANDARDS
for the Assessment
of Reading
and Writing

Prepared by
the Joint Task Force on Assessment
of the International Reading Association
and the National Council of Teachers of English

**National Council of
Teachers of English**

INTERNATIONAL
Reading Association
800 BARKSDALE ROAD, PO BOX 8139
NEWARK, DE 19714-8139, USA
www.reading.org

Cover Design   Linda Steere
IRA Stock number 776
NCTE Stock number   46864

Library of Congress Cataloging-in-Publication Data
Delaware. Task Force on Assessment of the International Reading Association.
  Standards for the assessment of reading and writing / Prepared by the Joint Task Force on Assessment of the International Reading Association and the National Council of Teachers of English.
-- Rev. ed.
     p. cm.
  Co-publication of the International Reading Association and the National Council of Teachers of English--Publisher.
  ISBN 978-0-87207-776-8
  1. Educational evaluation. 2. Language arts (Secondary) 3. Literature--Study and teaching (Secondary) I. International Reading Association. II. National Council of Teachers of English.
  LB2822.75.D44 2010
  379.1'58--dc22

                                                                                2009040109

The IRA–NCTE Joint Task Force on Assessment

The International Reading Association and the National Council of Teachers of English thank the following members of the Joint Task Force on Assessment for their work on this document.

Peter Johnston (chair)
The University at Albany, New York

Peter Afflerbach
University of Maryland, College Park

Sandra Krist
Los Angeles Unified School District, California

Kathryn Mitchell Pierce
Wydown Middle School, Clayton, Missouri

Elizabeth Spalding
University of Nevada, Las Vegas

Alfred W. Tatum
University of Illinois at Chicago

Sheila W. Valencia
University of Washington, Seattle

Introduction

This document provides a set of standards to guide decisions about assessing the teaching and learning of literacy. In the past 30 years, research has produced revolutionary changes in our understanding of language, learning, and the complex literacy demands of our rapidly changing society. The standards proposed in this document are intended to reflect these advances in our understanding.

Readers of this document most likely share common experiences with respect to literacy and assessment. For example, in our own school days, we were directed to read to get the correct meaning of a text so that we could answer questions put to us by someone who already knew that correct meaning or by a test (often multiple choice) for which the correct answers were already determined. In order to develop assessment practices that serve students in an increasingly complex society, we must outgrow the limitations of our own schooling histories and understand language, literacy, and assessment in more complex ways. Literacy involves not just reading and writing, but a wide range of related language activities. It is both more social and more personal than a mere set of skills.

The need to understand language is particularly important. Language is not only the object of assessment but also part of the process of assessment. Consequently, any discussion of literacy assessment must include a discussion of language—what it is, how it is learned, and how it relates to assessment. Before we state our assessment standards, then, we will give an overview of what we mean by assessment and how we understand language and its relationship to assessment.

The Nature of Assessment

For many years, a transmission view of knowledge, curriculum, and assessment dominated and appeared to satisfy our social, political, and economic needs. Knowledge was regarded as a static entity that was "out there" somewhere, so the key educational question was, How do you get it from out there into students' heads? The corollary assessment question was, What counts as evidence that the knowledge really is in their heads? In a transmission view, it made sense to develop educational standards that specified the content of instruction before developing assessment procedures and engagements.

In the 1920s, notions of the basic purposes of schooling began to shift from an emphasis on the transmission of knowledge to the more complex nurturing of independent and collaborative learning and of problem solving. This shift has gained increasing prominence in today's postindustrial society, with its ever-expanding need for workers with strong communication skills and dispositions toward problem solving and collaborating. A curriculum committed to independent learning is built on the premise that inquiry, rather than mere transmission of knowledge, is the basis of teaching and learning.

This shift from knowledge transmission to inquiry as a primary goal of schools has important implications for assessment. In a knowledge-transmission framework, tests of static knowledge can suffice as assessment instruments. Students are the participants who are primarily accountable (either they have the knowledge or they don't), with teachers held accountable next. Policymakers, including school board members, trustees, or regents, are the primary recipients of assessment data. An inquiry framework changes the role of assessment and the roles of the participants. Within this framework, assessment is the exploration of how the educational environment and the participants in the educational community support the process of students as they learn to become independent and collaborative thinkers and problem solvers. This exploration includes an examination of the environment for teaching and learning, the processes and products of learning, and the degree to which all participants—students, teachers, administrators, parents, and board members—meet their obligation to support inquiry. Such assessments examine not only learning over time but also the contexts of learning.

Inquiry emphasizes different processes and types of knowledge than does knowledge transmission. For example, it values the ability to recognize problems and to generate multiple and diverse perspectives in trying to solve them. An inquiry stance asserts that while knowledge and language are likely to change over time, the need for learners at all levels (students, teachers, parents, administrators, and policymakers) who can solve new problems, generate new knowledge, and invent new language practices will remain constant. An inquiry perspective promotes problem posing and problem solving as goals for all participants in the educational community. For example, inquiry values the question of how information from different sources can be used to solve a particular problem. It values explorations of how teachers can promote critical thinking for all students. And it raises the question of why our society privileges the knowledge and cultural heritage of some groups over others within current school settings.

Inquiry fits the needs of a multicultural society in which it is essential to value and find strength in cultural diversity. It also honors the commitment to raising questions and generating multiple solutions. Various stakeholders and cultural groups provide different answers and new perspectives on problems. Respecting difference among learners enriches the curriculum and reduces the likelihood of problematic curricular narrowing.

2

Just as the principle of inquiry values difference, so the principle of difference values conversation over recitation as the primary mode of discourse. In a recitation, it is assumed that one person, the teacher, possesses the answers and that the others, the students, interact with the teacher and one another in an attempt to uncover the teacher's knowledge. In a conversation, all of the stakeholders in the educational environment (students, parents, teachers, specialists, administrators, and policymakers) have a voice at the table as curriculum, standards, and assessments are negotiated. Neither inquiry nor learning is viewed as the exclusive domain of students and teachers; both are primary concerns for all members of the school community. For example, administrators ask themselves hard questions about whether the structures they have established support staff development, teacher reflection, and student learning. School board members ask themselves whether they have lived up to the standards they have set for themselves and their schools to provide teachers and students with the resources they need to guarantee learning opportunities.

Quality assessment, then, hinges on the process of setting up conditions so that the classroom, the school, and the community become centers of inquiry where students, teachers, and other members of the school community investigate their own learning, both individually and collaboratively. The onus of assessment does not fall disproportionately upon students and teachers (which is often the case in schools today); instead, all those inquiring into the nature and effectiveness of educational practices are responsible for investigating the roles they have played. Different members of the school community have different but interacting interests, roles, and responsibilities, and assessment is the medium that allows all to explore what they have learned and whether they have met their responsibilities to the school community.

The Nature of Language

Language is very much like a living organism. It cannot be put together from parts like a machine, and it is constantly changing. Like a living organism, it exists only in interaction with others, in a social interdependence. Language is a system of signs through and within which we represent and make sense of the world and of ourselves. Language does not contain meaning; rather, meaning is constructed in the social relationships within which language is used. Individuals make sense of language within their social relationships, their personal histories, and their collective memory. In order to make sense of even a single word, people take into account the situation and their relationship with the speaker or writer.

Take, for example, *family*, a word often used as if all members of society agree on its meaning. The word may mean different things in different contexts, however, whether cultural, situational, or personal. To a middle-aged white person whose parents moved across country with their two children and who repeated that experience herself, *family* may mean the nuclear family structure in which she grew up and in which she is raising her own children. To someone from a different culture—perhaps an African American or Asian American—the word may conjure images of the constellation of grandparents, aunts, uncles, and cousins who live together or near one another. So, meaning may vary from one person to another, as in this case, where meanings attached to the word *family* are likely to differ depending on one's own experience in the family or families one has lived with. Thus, individuals make different sense of apparently similar language to the extent that their cultural and personal histories do not coincide. Consequently, when we attempt to standardize a test (by making it the same for everyone), we make the tenuous assumption that students will all make the same meaning from the language of our instructions and the language of the individual items.

Different cultures also have different ways of representing the world, themselves, and their intentions with language. For example, in any given cultural group, people have different ways of greeting one another, depending on the situation (e.g., a business meeting, a funeral, a date) and on their relationship to each other. Our own language practices come from our cultural experience, but they are also part of the collective practice that forms the culture. Indeed, the different ways people use language to make sense of the world and of their lives are the major distinguishing features of different cultural groups.

At the same time, language is always changing as we use it. Words acquire different meanings, and new language structures and uses appear as people stretch and pull the language to make new meanings. Consequently, the meaning that individuals make from language varies across time, social situation, personal perspective, and cultural group.

The Nature of Literacy

The nature of literacy is also continually changing. Today, many children read more online than offline. They are growing into a digital world in which relatively little reading and writing involves paper, most reading and writing involves images as much as print, and writing (both formal and less formal, the latter including e-mail, texts, Facebook posts, etc.) is becoming equal to, or even supplanting, reading as a primary literacy engagement. The tools of literacy are changing rapidly as new forms of Internet communication technology (ICT) are created, including (at the time of writing) bulletin boards, Web editors, blogs, virtual worlds, and social networking sites such as Ning and MySpace. The social practices of literacy also change as a result of using digital technologies, as does the development of language. New literate practices are learned and refined just by existing from day to day in what has become known as the mediasphere. For example, living with cell phones leads to texting, which changes how people view writing and how they write, and frequenting Web 2.0 sites, such as the video-sharing service YouTube, privileges a visual mode and shapes both attention to and facility with other modes of meaning making. The literacies children encounter by the end of their schooling were unimagined when they began.

Reading and writing online changes what it means to read, write, and comprehend. Literacy practices now involve both the creation and use of multimodal texts (broadly defined). Creating multimodal texts requires knowing the properties and limitations of different digital tools so that decisions can be made about how best to serve one's intentions. Participating in social networking sites, for example, requires new literacy practices; new literacy practices shape how users are perceived and how they construct identities. This leads to new areas needing to be assessed, including how youths create and enhance multiple identities using digital tools and virtual spaces. We now need to be concerned with teaching and assessing how students take an idea in print and represent it with video clips for other audiences. Similarly, we must be concerned about the stances and practices involved in taking an idea presented in one modality (e.g., print) and transcribing or transmediating it into another (e.g., digital video), and we must consider what possibilities and limitations a particular mode offers and how that relates to its desirability over other modes for particular purposes and situations. Children use different comprehension strategies online and offline, and assessments of the two show different pictures of their literacy development. Online readers, by choosing hypertext and intertext links, actually construct the texts that they read as well as the meanings they make. New multimodal texts require new critical media literacies, linked to classical critical literacy notions of how media culture is created, appropriated, and subsequently colonizes the broader notions of culture—for example, how youth culture is defined by and used to define what youths do, what they buy, and with whom they associate.

The definitions of literacy that have dominated schooling and are insisted on by most current testing systems are inadequate for a new, highly networked information age. Failure to help all students acquire literacies for this age will not serve them or society well. Not to teach the necessary skills, strategies, dispositions, and social practices is to deny children full access to economic, social, and political participation in the new global society. Not to assess these capabilities will result in curricular neglect and a lack of information to inform instruction.

The Learning of Language

By the time children arrive at school, they have learned to speak at least one language and have mastered most of the language structures they will ever use. Through social interaction, using the language they hear around them from birth, they have developed, without their awareness, the underlying rules of grammar and the vocabulary that give meaning to the world as they see it. Nonetheless, we often teach language in schools as if children came to our classrooms with little or no language competence. Nothing could be further from the truth. Children can request, demand, explain, recount, persuade, and express opinions. They bring to school the ability to narrate their own life histories. They are authors creating meaning with language long before they arrive at school.

As children acquire language in social interaction, particularly with others whose language is different or more complex, they gain flexibility in using language for different purposes and in different social situations. Learning a second language or dialect roughly parallels learning the first, for learning any language also entails becoming competent in the social relationships that underlie it. Children also develop fluent use of language without explicit knowledge of or instruction in rules and grammars. This means that grammars and rules are taught most productively as tools for analyzing language after it has been acquired. Even adults who have considerable facility with the language frequently can articulate few, if any, grammar or language rules. In spite of this truism, we often go about assessment and instruction in schools as if this were not the case.

Furthermore, although we pretend otherwise, language is not acquired in any simple hierarchical sequence.

In some ways, school actually plays a modest role in language acquisition, the bulk of which occurs outside of school. In schools, we must learn to teach language in a way that preserves and respects individuality at the same time that we empower students to learn how to be responsible and responsive members of learning communities. In other words, we must respect their right to their own interpretations of language, including the texts they read and hear, but we must help them learn that meaning is negotiated with other members of the learning communities within which they live and work. To participate in that negotiation, they must understand and be able to master the language practices and means of negotiation of the cultures within which they live. They must understand the language conventions that are sanctioned in different social situations and the consequences of adhering to or violating those conventions.

Although much of our language is learned outside school, studying language is the foundation of all schooling, not just of the language arts. For example, in science class, we make knowledge of the world using language. To study science, then, we must study the language through which we make scientific knowledge, language that has an important impact on the curriculum. If in reading and writing about science the language is dispassionate and distancing, then that is part of the knowledge that students construct about science, part of the way they relate to the world through science.

The Assessment of Language

Our description of language and language learning has important implications for the assessment of language, first because it is the object of assessment (the thing being assessed) and second because it is the medium of assessment (the means through and within which we assess). Instructional outcomes in the language arts and assessment policies and practices should reflect what we know about language and its acquisition. For example, to base a test on the assumption that there is a single correct way to write a persuasive essay is a dubious practice. Persuading someone to buy a house is not the same as persuading someone to go on a date. Persuading someone in a less powerful position is not the same as persuading someone in a more powerful position—which is to say that persuasive practices differ across situations, purposes, and cultural groups. Similarly, that texts can (and should) be read from different perspectives must be taken as a certainty—a goal of schooling not to be disrupted by assessment practices that pretend otherwise. To assert through a multiple-choice test that a piece of text has only one meaning is unacceptable, given what we know of language.

Moreover, to the extent that assessment practices legitimize only the meanings and language practices of particular cultural groups, these practices are acts of cultural oppression. When our assessments give greater status to one kind of writing over another—for example, expository writing over narrative writing—we are making very powerful controlling statements about the legitimacy of particular ways of representing the world. These statements tend to be reflected in classroom practices.

When we attempt to document students' language development, we are partly involved in producing that development. For example, if we decide that certain skills are "basic" and some are "higher level," and that the former need to be acquired before the latter, that decision affects the way we organize classrooms, plan our teaching, group students, and discuss reading and writing with them. The way we teach literacy, the way we sequence lessons, the way we group students, even the way we physically arrange the classroom all have an impact on their learning.

The Language of Assessment

Because it involves language, assessment is an interpretive process. Just as we construct meanings for texts that we read and write, so do we construct "readings" or interpretations of our students based upon the many "texts" they provide for us. These assessment texts come in the form of the pieces that students write, their responses to literature, the various assignments and projects they complete, the contributions they make to discussions, their behavior in different settings, the questions they ask in the classroom or in conferences, their performances or demonstrations involving language use, and tests of their language competence. Two different people assessing a student's reading or writing, his or her literate development, may use different words to describe it.

In classrooms, teachers assess students' writing and reading and make evaluative comments about writers whose work is read. The language of this classroom assessment becomes the language of the literate classroom community and thus becomes the language through which students evaluate their own reading and writing. If the language of classroom assessment implies that there are several interpretations of any particular text, students will come to gain confidence as they assess their own interpretations and will value diversity in the classroom. If, on the other hand, the language of classroom assessment implies that reading and writing can be reduced to a simple continuum of quality, students will assess their own literacy only in terms of their place on that continuum relative to other students, without reflecting productively on their own reading and writing practices.

When teachers write report cards, they are faced with difficult language decisions. They must find words to represent a student's literate development in all its complexity, often within severe time, space, and format constraints. They must also accomplish this within the diverse relationships and cultural backgrounds among the parents, students, and administrators who might read the reports. Some teachers are faced with reducing extensive and complex knowledge about each student's development to a single word or letter. This situation confronts them with very difficult ethical dilemmas. Indeed, the greater the knowledge the teacher has of the student's literacy, the more difficult this task becomes.

But it is not just classroom assessment that is interpretive. The public "reads" students, teachers, and schools from the data that are provided. Parents make sense of a test score or a report card grade or comment based on their own schooling history, beliefs, and values. A test score may look "scientific" and "objective," but it too must be interpreted, which is always a subjective and value-laden process.

The terms with which people discuss students' literacy development have also changed over time. For example, in recent history, students considered to be having difficulty becoming literate have acquired different labels, such as *basic writer, remedial reader, disadvantaged, learning disabled, underachiever, struggling student,* or *retarded reader.* These different terms can have quite different consequences. Students described as "learning disabled" are often treated and taught quite differently from students who are similarly literate but described as "remedial readers."

Further, assessment itself is the object of much discussion, and the language of that discussion is also important. For example, teachers' observations are often described as informal and subjective and contrasted with test results that are considered "formal" and "objective." The knowledge constructed in a discussion that uses these terms would be quite different from that constructed in a discussion in which teachers' observations were described as "direct documentation" and test results as "indirect estimation."

Assessment terms change as different groups appropriate them for different purposes and as situations change. Recent discussions about assessment have changed some of the ways in which previously reasonably predictable words are used, belying the simplicity of the glossary we include at the end of this document. For example, the term *norm-referenced* once meant that assessment data on one student, typically test data, were interpreted in comparison with the data on other students who were considered similar. A norm-referenced interpretation of a student's writing might assert that it is "as good as that of 20 percent of the students that age in the country." Similarly, the term *criterion-referenced assessment* once meant simply that a student's performance was interpreted with respect to a particular level of performance—either it met the criterion or it did not. Recently, however, it has become much less clear how these terms are being used. The line between criterion and norm has broken down. For example, *criterion* has recently come to mean "dimension" or "valued characteristic." *Norm* has come to be used in much the same sense. But even in the earlier (and still more common) meaning, most criteria for criterion-referenced tests are arrived at by finding out how a group of students performs on the test and then setting criteria in accord with what seems a reasonable point for a student's passing or failing the test.

In other words, assessment is never merely a technical process. Assessment is always representational and interpretive because it involves representing children's development. Assessment practices shape the ways we see children, how they see themselves, and how they engage in future learning. Assessment is social and, because of its consequences, political. As with other such socially consequential practices, it is necessary to have standards against which practitioners can judge the responsibility of their practices.

Using This Document

In what follows, each standard is presented as a statement with a brief explanatory paragraph. The standard is then expanded with additional detail. The text concludes with case studies that illustrate the standards' implications in both large-scale and classroom assessments.

The central premise of the standards is that quality assessment is a process of inquiry. It requires gathering information and setting conditions so that the classroom, the school, and the community become centers of inquiry where students, teachers, and other members of the school community examine, individually and collaboratively, their learning and ways to improve their practice.

The Standards

1. The interests of the student are paramount in assessment.

Assessment experiences at all levels, whether formative or summative, have consequences for students (see standard 7). Assessments may alter their educational opportunities, increase or decrease their motivation to learn, elicit positive or negative feelings about themselves and others, and influence their understanding of what it means to be literate, educated, or successful. It is not enough for assessment to serve the well-being of students "on average"; we must aim for assessment to serve, not harm, each and every student.

The following assessment practices are most likely to serve students' interests. First and foremost, assessment must encourage students to become engaged in literacy learning, to reflect on their own reading and writing in productive ways, and to set respective literacy goals. In this way, students become involved in, and responsible for, their own learning and are better able to assist the teacher in focusing instruction. Some assessment practices, however, such as those that include public comparisons of students, tend to produce conditions of threat and defensiveness, limiting students' engagement and their ability to reflect productively on their performance. English-language learners face a double hurdle, since their test results often reflect both their knowledge of a subject and their knowledge of the English language. Constructive reflection is particularly difficult under such conditions. Thus, assessment should emphasize what students can do rather than what they cannot do. Portfolio assessment, for example, if managed properly, can be reflective, involving students in their own learning and assisting teachers in refocusing their instruction.

Assessments that serve the students' interests might include many of the multimodal texts that students create outside of school because they are constructed for purposes that the students establish—for example, how they update their MySpace pages based on their interests, recent events, or new friends. Most of the texts they create as artifacts of typical reading of print in school are for purposes established by teachers. It is possible that we could get much more valid assessments of their literacy practices if we provided more opportunities for them to select both texts (whether print or multimodal) and tools (e.g., Web 2.0 tools).

Second, assessment must provide useful information to inform and enable reflection. The information must be both specific and timely. Specific information on students' knowledge, skills, strategies, and attitudes helps teachers, parents, and students set goals and plan instruction more thoughtfully. Information about students' confusions, counterproductive strategies, and limitations, too, can help students and teachers reflect on and learn about students' reading and writing, as long as it is provided in the context of clear descriptions of what they can do. It is equally important that assessments provide timely information. If information is not provided immediately, it is not likely to be used, nor is it likely to be useful because needs, interests, and aspirations generally change with the passage of time. In either case, the opportunity to influence and promote learning may be missed.

Third, the assessment must yield high-quality information. The quality of information is suspect when tasks are too difficult or too easy, when students do not understand the tasks or cannot follow the directions, or when they are too anxious to be able to do their best or even their typical work. In these situations, students cannot produce their best efforts or demonstrate what they know. For example, researchers have found that modifying or simplifying the language of test items has consistently resulted in English-language learners' improved performance and does not sacrifice the rigor of the test. Requiring students to spend their time and efforts on assessment tasks that do not yield high-quality, useful information results in students losing valuable learning time. Such a loss does not serve their interests and thus constitutes an invalid practice (see standard 7).

It is important to note that many classroom-level assessments also fail to meet criteria for serving student interests. Regardless of the source or motivation for any particular assessment, states, school districts, schools, and teachers must demonstrate how the assessment practices benefit and do not harm individual students.

This standard requires that if any individual student's interests are not served by an assessment practice, regardless of whether it is intended for administration or decision making by an individual or by a group (as is the case with tests used to apply accountability pressure on teachers), then that practice is not valid for that student. Those responsible for requiring an assessment are responsible for demonstrating how these assessment practices benefit and do not harm individual students.

Traditionally, group-administered, machine-scorable tests have not encouraged students to reflect constructively on their reading and writing, have not provided specific and timely feedback, and generally have not provided high-quality information about students. Consequently, they have seemed unlikely to serve the best interests of students. However, this need not be the case if they are able to provide timely, high-quality information to students.

Assessment instruments or procedures themselves are not the only consideration in this standard. The context in which they are used can be equally important. Indeed, the most productive and powerful assessments for students are likely to be the formative assessments that occur in the daily activities of the classroom. Maximizing the value of these for students and minimizing the likelihood that they are damaging for any one student might involve an investment in staff development and the creation of conditions that enable teachers to reflect on their own practice. Similarly, assessment by portfolio might work well when teachers have expertise in a workshop approach to literacy but not when there is pressure for performance on a high-stakes multiple-choice test. This is not to say that portfolio assessment that satisfies this standard in the classroom may not also satisfy it in the context of a high-stakes assessment, such as an accountability assessment.

2. The teacher is the most important agent of assessment.

Most educational assessment takes place in the classroom, as teachers and students interact with one another. Teachers design, assign, observe, collaborate in, and interpret the work of students in their classrooms. They assign meaning to interactions and evaluate the information that they receive and create in these settings. In short, teachers are the primary agents, not passive consumers, of assessment information. It is their ongoing, formative assessments that primarily influence students' learning. This standard acknowledges the critical role of the teacher and the consequences and responsibilities that accompany this role.

Whether they use tests, work samples, discussion, or ongoing observation, teachers make sense of students' reading and writing development. They read these many different texts, oral and written, that students produce in order to construct an understanding of students as literate individuals. The sense they make of a student's reading or writing is communicated to the student through spoken or written comments and translated into instructional decisions in the classroom (e.g., subsequent assignments, grouping for instruction). Because of such important consequences, teachers must be aware of and deliberate about their roles as assessors.

This responsibility demands considerable expertise. First, unless teachers can recognize the significance of aspects of a student's performance—a particular kind of error or behavior, for example—they will be unable to adjust instruction accordingly. They must know what signs to attend to in children's literate behavior. This requires a deep knowledge of the skills and processes of reading and writing and a sound understanding of their own literacy practices. Therefore, it is important that teachers themselves be readers and writers who understand these processes from the inside out. The more knowledgeable teachers are on the subjects of reading and writing and the more observant they are of students' literate behavior, the more productive their assessments will be. It is particularly important that teachers who work with English-language learners possess the specific knowledge and skills required to recognize students' developing proficiency and help them become fully literate.

Second, teachers must have routines for systematic assessment in order to ensure that each student is benefiting optimally from instruction.

Third, because of the need for this level of expertise and because the quality of formative assessment has a strong effect on the quality of instruction, improving teachers' assessment expertise requires ongoing professional development, coaching, and access to professional learning communities. Nurturing such communities must be a priority for improving assessment. Teachers need to feel safe to share, discuss, and critique their own work in public forums with their peers. These conditions encourage the engagement of the multiple perspectives necessary both for learning and for reducing the effects of individual biases.

Fourth, as agents of assessment, teachers must take responsibility for making and sharing judgments about students' achievements and progress. They cannot defer to others or to other instruments. At the same time, others must come to trust and support teachers in their judgments. Such trust and support are fostered when school communities are organized in ways that bring multiple perspectives to the assessment process and counter any inherent bias (see standard 5).

Fifth, much of the assessment information in classrooms is made available in students' talk about their reading and writing. When students have conversations about a book, for instance, a teacher hears the process of their comprehending. Unless a teacher can generate such conversations among children, this information is simply not available.

Unlike makers of standardized tests, teachers are in a unique position to engage in valid assessment. Because they are closest to students' learning, they have the opportunity to make many detailed observations over time. For example, the use of classroom portfolios can reduce the likelihood that a student's "bad day" performance will unduly influence a teacher's conclusions about that student's overall literacy. Classroom portfolios also allow a wider range of observations to be made in more diverse and representative situations, thus increasing the validity of the assessments. Teachers can adapt assessments to the special characteristics of individual students, instructional programs, and community expectations, as well as using their assessments to reflect on the effectiveness of their own instructional practice.

Superficially, commercially published tests appear to offer an objectivity that teachers' classroom assessments may lack. In reality, our understanding of language asserts that it is not possible to construct an unbiased test of literacy. The basis for less-biased assessment repertoires is teachers' knowledge about learning and literacy. The foundation of this assessment ability is deep and diverse knowledge of individual students and of reading and writing. The more teachers know about literacy development in general and, more important, about the literacy development of individual students, the more insightful they will be about understanding students' literate practices and the better equipped they will be to provide appropriate instruction.

Teacher knowledge cannot be replaced by standardized tests. Any one-shot assessment procedure cannot capture the depth and breadth of information teachers have available to them. Even when a widely used, commercial test is administered, teachers must draw upon the full range of their knowledge about content and individual students to make sense of the limited information such a test provides. A teacher who knows a great deal about the range of techniques readers and writers use will be able to provide students and other audiences with specific, focused feedback about learning. Indeed, students learn things about themselves and about literacy from teachers' feedback that no standardized test can supply. Most standardized tests compare students to one another, while teachers' comments can be specific and individualized, providing a clear picture of each student's special strengths and weaknesses. Students can then use such feedback in their self-evaluations. When students are able to engage in self-evaluation, they are more likely to take control of their own literate learning.

3. The primary purpose of assessment is to improve teaching and learning.

Assessment is used in educational settings for a variety of purposes, such as keeping track of learning, diagnosing reading and writing difficulties, determining eligibility for programs, evaluating programs, evaluating teaching, and reporting to others. Underlying all these purposes is a basic concern for improving teaching and learning. In the United States it is common to use testing for accountability, but the ultimate goal remains the improvement of teaching and learning. Similarly, we use assessments to determine eligibility for special education services, but the goal is more appropriate teaching and better learning for particular students. In both cases, if improved teaching and learning do not result, the assessment practices are not valid (see standard 7).

If an educational assessment practice is to be considered valid, it must inform instruction and lead to improved teaching and learning. The assessment problem then becomes one of setting conditions so that classrooms and schools become centers of inquiry where students and teachers investigate and improve their own learning and teaching practices, both individually and as learning communities. This in turn requires teachers, schools, and school districts not only to use assessment to reflect on learning and teaching but also to examine, constantly and critically, the assessment process itself and its relation to instruction. No matter how elaborate and precise the data provided by an assessment procedure are, its interpretation, its use, or the context of its use can render it useless or worse with respect to improving teaching and learning. For example, climates in which perfectly useful assessment data are employed to place blame can lead to defensiveness rather than to problem solving and improved learning.

Ensuring that assessment leads to the improvement of teaching and learning is not simply a technical matter of devising instruments for generating higher quality data. At least as important are the conditions under which assessment takes place and the climate produced by assessment practices. Sometimes the language we choose to frame assessment distracts us from this standard. We believe that the commonly expressed need for "higher standards" is better expressed as the need for higher quality instruction, for without it, higher standards simply means denying greater numbers of students access to programs and opportunities. The central function of assessment, therefore, is not to prove whether teaching or learning has taken place, but to improve the quality of teaching and learning and thereby to increase the likelihood that all members of the society will acquire a full and critical literacy (see standard 1).

4. Assessment must reflect and allow for critical inquiry into curriculum and instruction.

Sound educational practices start with a curriculum that values complex literacy, instructional practices that nurture it, and assessments that fully reflect it. In order for assessment to allow productive inquiry into curriculum and instruction, it must reflect the complexity of that curriculum as well as the instructional practices in schools. This is particularly important because assessment shapes teaching, learning, and policy. Assessment that reflects an impoverished view of literacy will result in a diminished curriculum and distorted instruction and will not enable productive problem solving or instructional improvement. Because assessment shapes instruction, the higher the stakes of the assessment, the more important it is that it reflect this full complexity.

Critical inquiry into curriculum, instruction, and assessment is important at all levels. Policymakers, no less than teachers and students, must have clear understandings of the curriculum and instructional practices in order to make informed decisions. Decisions based on severely restricted or distorted information or on unexamined assumptions will be poor decisions.

Two major problems beset efforts to inquire into curriculum, instruction, and assessment. The first is that reading and writing standards guiding curricula in many districts often fragment literacy rather than represent its complexity. They also frequently omit important aspects of literacy such as self-initiated learning, questioning author's bias, perspective taking, multiple literacies, social interactions around literacy, metacognitive strategies, and literacy dispositions. Furthermore, even when the standards come closer to representing these features of complex literacy, high-stakes assessments rarely address the difficult-to-measure standards, opting instead to focus on content that is easier and more expedient to assess using inexpensive test formats. For example, teachers who emphasize the clarity of writing, attention to audience, vibrant language, revision, and sound support of assertions advocated in many content standards rarely find such qualities fully reflected in high-stakes tests, or they find these standards assessed through items that focus on mechanics or conventions. Similarly, students who are urged in classroom instruction to form opinions and back them up need to be assessed accordingly, rather than with tests that do not allow for creative or divergent thinking.

A second, related problem is the power of assessments to shape instruction (see standard 7). Pressure associated with high-stakes tests as well as some forms of progress monitoring have focused attention on implementing specific curriculum programs, interventions, or approaches to instruction. Instructional practices such as providing additional support for students who perform just below cut scores ("bubble kids"), but not for those significantly below, or efforts to increase reading rate without regard for comprehension, should be questioned. Other measures of opportunity to learn, such as teachers' access to ongoing professional development and the availability of resources to connect schools to local communities, must also be considered.

Policymakers and administrators, no less than teachers and students, have a responsibility to understand the complexities and importance of a full and critical literacy and the nature of instruction that will foster it. They must recognize that tests, although sometimes necessary, are often not the best assessment procedures for capturing the subtleties of teaching and learning. They must recognize test results for what they obscure or fail to assess as well as for what they reveal. In the public interest, they must not endow test scores with the power to tell more than they are able. Hundreds of studies have shown that nonschool factors, such as parents' education level or socioeconomic status, have a greater effect on student achievement than do school factors. Tests that do not adequately reflect a complex model of literacy send a misleading message to teachers and students about the kinds of reading and writing that are valued by society.

In sum, without critical inquiry into the link between specific assessments and curricula, it is difficult to know whether an assessment provides a full representation of literacy or even represents a valid measure of the standards it is intended to represent.

5. Assessment must recognize and reflect the intellectually and socially complex nature of reading and writing and the important roles of school, home, and society in literacy development.

Literacy is complex, social, and constantly changing. The literacies of students graduating from high school today were barely imaginable when they began their schooling. Outside of school, students live and will go on to work in a media culture with practices unlike those currently occurring in school (even in the setting of the school media center). Students need to acquire competencies with word processors, blogs, wikis, Web browsers, instant messaging, listservs, bulletin boards, virtual worlds, video editors, presentation software, and many other literate tools and practices. Traditional, simple definitions of literacy will not help prepare students for the literate lives of the present—let alone the future. Consequently, reading and writing cannot usefully be assessed as a set of isolated, independent tasks or events. It is critical to gather specific information about materials, tasks, and media being used with students for both instructional and assessment purposes. In addition, we need to assess how practices are used to participate in the broader media culture as well as to examine how the broader culture assigns status to some practices over others (e.g., texting as contrasted to writing paragraph summaries in language arts class).

Whatever the medium, literacy is social and involves negotiations among authors and readers around meanings, purposes, and contexts. Literate practices are now rarely solitary cognitive acts. Furthermore, literate practices differ across social and cultural contexts and across different media. Students' behavior in one setting may not be at all representative of their behavior in another. This may be particularly true of English-language learners who may lack the fluency to express themselves fully inside the classroom but may be lively contributors in their families and communities.

In school settings, instruction and assessment should be seen as highly interactive processes. For example, aspects of the learning situation interact with cultural and home environments to influence student learning and motivation. These social situations shape purposes for both teachers and students, influence the conditions and constraints present in the learning context, and affect students' motivation to engage in reading and writing activities. In the social context of schooling, many factors influence learning and performance. These include types of activities, management efficiency, grouping patterns, teacher and student expectations and beliefs, classroom interactions, and the classroom environment. In addition, factors associated with teaching, such as content, tasks, and materials, all affect literacy learning.

The quality and appropriateness of assessment efforts depend to a considerable extent on the degree to which these complexities have been considered. The quality of an assessment will be low if it yields an incomplete or distorted picture of a student's literacy. Characteristics of the text, the task, the situation, and the purpose can all have an impact on the student's performance, and only some aspects of reading and writing will be captured in any given assessment situation. Formal tests need to be considerably more complex than is generally true today. Tests that accommodate multiple responses, different types of texts and tasks, and indicators of attitude and motivation are all essential to a comprehensive view of literacy achievement. Wherever possible, assessments must specify the types of texts, tasks, and situations used for assessment purposes and note whether and when students' performance was improved by variations in text quality, type of task, or situation.

In order to meet this standard, we must depend less on one-shot assessment practices and place more value on assessments of ongoing classroom performance, assuming that classroom curricula develop the full complexity of literate learning. Finally, when assessment information is interpreted and reported, descriptive information about the assessment tasks and texts and the instructional situation should be included. Given the complexity of the tasks involved, reducing reading and writing performance to a letter or number grade is unacceptable.

6. Assessment must be fair and equitable.

We live in a multicultural society with laws that promise equal rights to all. Our school communities must work to ensure that all students, as different as they are in cultural, ethnic, religious, linguistic, and economic background, receive a fair and equitable education. Assessment plays an important part in ensuring fairness and equity, first, because it is intimately related to curriculum, instruction, and learning, and second, because assessment provides a seemingly impartial way of determining who should and who should not be given access to educational institutions and resources. To be fair, then, assessment must be as free as possible of biases based on ethnic group, gender, nationality, religion, socioeconomic condition, sexual orientation, or disability. Furthermore, assessment must help us to confront biases that exist in schooling.

In the past, standardized tests have been viewed as a means to avoid the cultural and personal biases of teachers' judgments. However, just as it is impossible to eliminate bias from teachers, it is also impossible to produce an unbiased test of reading or writing. Language itself involves social conventions that differ from culture to culture. Furthermore, words have different shades of meaning for different cultures, and the variation in life experiences across culturally, economically, and geographically different situations can be quite extreme. Consequently, students differ enormously in the interpretations they give to the texts they read, the topics they feel comfortable writing about, and the ways they respond to different forms of assessment. The curriculum-distorting effects of high-stakes testing are also distributed unevenly across subgroups of the population. In the United States, urban schools with significant numbers of students living in poverty are more subject to the curriculum-narrowing pressures of high-stakes testing than are more affluent suburban schools.

The inevitability of bias notwithstanding, when tests must be used, as many biases as possible should be controlled. Whenever possible, assessment should be accomplished in a language that will not interfere with the individual's performance. Assessment practices should not devalue cultural differences in dialect. Students have the right to learn the language of the dominant culture because it is the language of power. However, students should not be penalized in assessments for using their home language where the privileged dialect is not specifically required. Assessment must also take into consideration the differences between basic and academic language and the length of time students need to become skilled at each.

Biases routinely occur in assessments and in the curricula they represent. For example, all students should study and be assessed on literature from and knowledge of cultures other than their own. Failure to do so introduces a cultural bias. However, there are other biases that regularly occur as a result of assessments. Students who are initially less successful than others in literacy acquisition often find that their curriculum shrinks to one that is less engaging and less mind-expanding. This form of bias is often also associated with economic differences across schools, and it perpetuates those differences by reducing the breadth and complexity of the literacy students acquire. Assessment that allows for critical inquiry into the curriculum is an important antidote to such common but avoidable inequalities and also serves to make institutional biases clear and public.

Most biases are part of the perspective we bring from our cultural backgrounds, so we tend not to notice them in ourselves. We must strive to have the testing industry, policymakers, administrators, and teachers—all those charged with creating and interpreting tests—reflect and respect the diversity of our society. At the same time, it is particularly important that multiple perspectives be brought to bear on assessment issues (see standard 8). One way to take test bias seriously would be to ensure strong and varied representation of culturally, ethnically, linguistically, and economically diverse groups in the construction of public tests. In this way, test biases should become apparent and, once recognized, be easier to reduce. A second important way to address bias is to make tests available for public examination after they have been given. A third way to offset bias is to ensure that no single assessment is used to make important educational decisions (see standard 8).

Inequities in schooling can also be compounded through inappropriate assessment. For example, assessment practices, both large scale and centered in the classroom, often lead to students being placed in different instructional settings or programs with the intention of producing a better match between student and curriculum. This leads to a significant equity issue. On the one hand, a better instructional match is possible, but on the other, different and perhaps lowered expectations on the parts of both teachers and students themselves may result. Once students are assigned to systematically different curricula, uneven access to subsequent experiences and jobs becomes not just possible, but probable.

Other uses of assessments can also produce inequities. For example, external pressures regarding the use of tests often differ across school settings within individual districts or specific regions. This is particularly common in large cities. Similarly, a common practice in newspapers in some areas is to report the average test scores of students by district, school, or even classroom. Because individuals and businesses are reluctant to move into areas where schools have low scores on tests, tax bases and economic resources erode in these neighborhoods with the result that economically stressed school systems become more so. Pressure on teachers also increases, which creates greater teacher attrition and leaves high-needs schools with a less experienced teaching force.

When assessing, we must be sure to attend to the relevant competencies. For example, provisions should be made to ensure that second-language learners are assessed in ways that permit them to show what they know and can do, with consideration for the time it takes to develop both basic and academic language. For students classified as reading disabled, the situation is less clear. In some U.S. states it is considered appropriate for these students to have their reading assessments read aloud to them. This practice may seem fair, but it makes productive inquiry impossible because the assessment no longer represents the construct "reading."

We must also remember that, although assessment plays an important role in ensuring fairness and equity, the goal of equity cannot be laid solely at the feet of assessment. No assessment practice can shore up the differences in educational experience that arise from the obviously unequal conditions of extreme poverty and wealth.

7. The consequences of an assessment procedure are the first and most important consideration in establishing the validity of the assessment.

Tests, checklists, observation schedules, and other assessments cannot be evaluated out of the context of their use. If a perfectly reliable and comprehensive literacy test were designed but using it took three weeks away from children's learning and half the annual budget for instructional materials, we would have to weigh these consequences against any value gained from using the test. If its use resulted in teachers building a productive learning community around the data and making important changes in their instruction, we would also have to weigh these consequences. This standard essentially argues for "environmental impact" projections, along with careful, ongoing analyses of the consequences of assessment practices. Responsibility for this standard lies with the entire school community, to ensure that assessments are not used in ways that have negative consequences for schools and students. Any assessment procedure that does not contribute positively to teaching and learning should not be used.

By asserting that procedures cannot be evaluated out of the context of their use, this standard puts assessment, teaching, and learning back together. It asserts that simply devising a more detailed or more complex test will not by itself result in a more valid assessment. If an assessment procedure has adverse motivational consequences for school communities, segments of school communities, or individuals, then the procedure is invalid.

Adverse consequences from assessment can arise in a variety of ways, such as in these examples:

- Assessment techniques that very publicly value only a narrow range of literacy activity or very controlling forms of reading and writing (as opposed to a more critical literacy) enforce a narrowing of the curriculum for students. This routinely occurs in the United States through high-stakes accountability testing. Classroom assessment practices can have the same effects, sometimes as a consequence of high-stakes testing practices. This occurs when, for example, classroom assessment focuses on worksheets and multiple-choice tests or when evaluative feedback on student writing focuses on spelling and grammar and not on students' thinking, substantive content, or organization or when classroom assessment focuses centrally on reading speed.

- Institutionally enforced commercial assessments reduce available school resources for teachers to conduct more instructionally informative assessments.

- Reporting procedures that focus on ranking or rating rather than on performance draw learners' attention away from the process of learning, reduce their notions of literacy acquisition to a simple linear continuum, disrupt collaborative learning communities, make students and teachers defensive, and thus inhibit learning.

This standard rejects the unfortunately common argument that a given test is valid in spite of the fact that its use has problematic consequences (e.g., placing a student in a program that does not serve her well). Inquiring into the effects of assessment practices is never simple. It should be ongoing, capitalizing on multiple data sources and multiple perspectives, always recognizing that these efforts are likely to raise value-laden conflicts, such as the tension between the public's right to know and the preservation of conditions that will foster learning. This standard means that assessment information should not be used for judgmental or political purposes if that would be likely to cause harm to students or to the effectiveness of teachers or schools. Schools have a responsibility to report assessment results to parents in a way that will assist, not hinder, students' learning and parents' understanding.

It is commonplace to talk about different purposes for assessment and to invoke the principle that the assessment must match the purpose for which it is intended. In practice, this has been largely ignored. Test publishers make claims regarding the validity of their tests regardless of the use to which they are put. In light of what we have learned about the ways tests shape curricular decisions made about students by teachers, administrators, and policymakers, a "user beware" attitude is unacceptable within the framework of this standard. If assessments are to be used for high-stakes purposes such as holding people publicly accountable, then they should be fully consistent with, and not a shorthand for, the assessment procedures used to provide teachers and students with knowledge of progress in the classroom. They must recognize the complexity of literacy in today's society (see standard 5) and reflect the curriculum.

This standard has implications for our priorities when we choose assessment practices. For example, when a teacher observes and documents a student's oral reading behaviors and uses that information to inform instruction, the data might not be as reliable, in a technical sense, as a norm-referenced test. However, in the context of the teacher's professional knowledge, they are more likely to have productive consequences. Often assessments are chosen for technical measurement properties rather than for the likelihood of productive consequences for students and teachers.

8. The assessment process should involve multiple perspectives and sources of data.

Perfect assessments and perfect assessors do not exist. Every person involved in assessment is limited in his or her interpretation of the teaching and learning of reading and writing. Similarly, each text and each assessment procedure has its own limitations and biases. Although we cannot totally eliminate these biases and limitations from people or tests, we can try to ensure that they are held in balance and that all stakeholders are made aware of them. The more consequential the decision, the more important it is to seek diverse perspectives and independent sources of data. For example, decisions about placement in or eligibility for specialized programs have a profound influence on a student's life and learning. Such decisions are simply too important to make on the basis of a single measure, evaluation tool, or perspective.

The need for multiple indicators is particularly important in assessing reading and writing because of the complex nature of literacy and its acquisition (see standard 5). A single measure is likely to be misleading or erroneous for individuals or groups. For example, timed essay tests of writing can significantly underpredict the ability of English-language learners to write under natural conditions, and instructional decisions made on the basis of results on such tests will thus impede their educational progress. Multiple sources of data, on the other hand, can allow for triangulation in problem solving. Sources of data can include observations made in different situations or by different people at different times or data from different assessment instruments. However, data from more than one of the same kind of assessment instrument (for example, a series of standardized tests) will not satisfy this standard because such tests commonly reflect a similar and narrow view of literacy. By the same token, even new data can be looked at with old eyes. Unless different perspectives and values are brought to bear on data, our understanding might not expand. Even the richest set of data can be reduced to mere conventions by a limited perspective.

From a more statistical point of view, the reliability of interpretations of assessment data is likely to improve when there are multiple opportunities to observe reading and writing. Adherence to this standard will also substantially improve the validity of the literacy assessment process because sampling more than one aspect of literacy permits a closer approximation of the complexity of reading, writing, listening, and speaking processes as they occur and as they are used in real-life settings.

However, seeking multiple perspectives and sources of data is not intended only for the purposes of reducing biases or errors in individual data sources. Instead, it takes advantage of the depth of understanding that varied assessment perspectives afford and the dialogue and learning they produce. Two teachers with different cultural or linguistic backgrounds might interpret a student's literacy development in different ways, each of which provides an important perspective. Indeed, because literacy learning is also social in nature, these two teachers' different interpretations will lead to different kinds of development. The exploration of these contrasting perspectives will lead not only to a more productive understanding of the specific student's development but also to an enhanced awareness of possible interpretations of other students' development— and of what it means to develop.

9. Assessment must be based in the local school learning community, including active and essential participation of families and community members.

The teacher is the primary agent of assessment and the classroom is the location of the most important assessment practices, but the most effective assessment unit is the local school learning community. First, the collective experience and values of the community can offer a sounding board for innovation and multiple perspectives to provide depth of understanding and to counter individual and cultural biases. Second, the involvement of all parties in assessment encourages a cooperative, committed relationship among them rather than an adversarial one. Third, because language learning is not restricted to what occurs in school, assessment must go beyond the school curriculum.

The local school learning community is also a more appropriate foundation for assessment than larger units such as the school district, county, state, province, or country. These larger units do not offer the relational possibilities and commitments necessary for a learning community. The distance from the problems to be solved and among the participants reduces the probability of feelings of involvement and commitment and increases the possibility that assessment will become merely a means of placing blame.

With the school community as a center of inquiry, diversity of perspective is possible not only as a source of growth for individual classrooms and teachers but also among teachers, administrators, and more broadly among stakeholders. Diversity of perspective brings depth of understanding and productive problem solving, and face-to-face involvement brings personal knowledge of the issues of assessment as well as personal investment in them. If teachers are able to make informed assessments and articulate them well, it is largely because they have been engaged in dialogue about their students' reading, writing, and learning and have been supported by the larger community in doing so. In order for a school community to do this effectively, it is necessary to engage in self-examination and make learning with the community a priority.

To function as a center of inquiry, a school must develop a trusting relationship with its community. This relationship commonly grows by involving all members of the community, balancing power, and recognizing different points of view. Because building such a relationship is nearly impossible in the context of large schools (whose hierarchical structures discourage the openness necessary for reflection, discussion, and inquiry), manageable schools-within-schools become an important possibility to be considered.

Schools have a responsibility to help families and community members understand the assessment process and the range of tools that can be useful in painting a detailed picture of learning, including both how individual students are learning and how the school is doing in its efforts to support learning. A part of this educational process must also be helping families and the local community to understand the most effective and appropriate uses of a variety of assessment tools, including large-scale standardized achievement tests.

There must be an ethos that educators are learners too, particularly about their own role in students' learning and the operation of their institutions. In order for educators to learn from others' perspectives, school communities bear particular responsibility for ensuring that all their members become fully involved in the assessment process. Many parents and caregivers, partly because of cultural disparities, linguistic barriers, or their own schooling histories, do not feel comfortable voicing their concerns. School communities have a responsibility to create conditions and assessment procedures that make people comfortable doing so.

As families become more fully involved in schools and assessments, they become more informed about and more observant of their children's development. This involvement allows them to be more supportive of their children's learning and of teachers' efforts and leads them to articulate more clearly their concerns about their children's progress. When families are intimately involved in the assessment process, they are less likely to allow cultural or racial bias to interfere in their efforts to determine how well their children are learning and how well their schools are doing. Furthermore, when administrators, families, and the public become involved together in assessment issues, trusting relationships are likely to evolve. With a trusting relationship, members of the school community can confront limitations and weaknesses as well as recognize strengths of their curriculum and assessments.

Parents and caregivers know a great deal about their children's learning and have an important perspective to add to local conversations about assessment. Schools must engage parents and the local community in conversations about the goals they have for the ways children will use reading and writing and the ways reading and writing are used in the community. When parents and the local community are intimately involved in the assessment of learning, they are in a better position to understand the assessment information reported and better able to support the literacy learning of children.

10. All stakeholders in the educational community—students, families, teachers, administrators, policymakers, and the public—must have an equal voice in the development, interpretation, and reporting of assessment information.

Each of the constituents named in this standard has a stake in assessment. Students are concerned because their literacy learning, their concepts of themselves as literate people, and the quality of their subsequent lives and careers are at stake. Teachers have at stake their understandings of their students, their professional practice and knowledge, their perceptions of themselves as teachers, and the quality of their work life and standing in the community. Families clearly have an investment in their children's learning, well-being, and educational future. The public invests money in education, in part as an investment in the future, and has a stake in maintaining the quality of that investment. The stewardship of the investment involves administrators and policymakers. Assessment is always value laden, and the ongoing participation of all parties involved in it is necessary in a democratic society. When any one perspective is missing, silenced, or privileged above others, the assessment picture is distorted.

Stakeholders closest to the process—families, teachers, students, and the local community—are most familiar with the intimate details of children's learning and are in the best position to observe and document the small, yet important, steps that make up learning. These intimate participants in the process have access to information about a child's growth over time, how a child is developing skill in the processes of learning that will lead to more learning in the future, and how a child is applying prior learning in new situations. Following public laws in most countries, policymakers have the responsibility of ensuring equity and preventing local injustices.

However, when policymakers develop practices that drive local assessment and instructional processes, other stakeholders' voices are easily silenced and assessment becomes dominated by procedures developed by people who have little regular contact with students or teachers. Policy has always privileged some forms of literacy over others, but today the privileged forms generally exclude genres and modalities that children increasingly use—webpages, social networking sites, texting, and so on—and that are increasingly required beyond school. It may be possible to get more valid data on traditional assessments, even large-scale assessments, if the content and modalities of the assessments are adapted to students' interests in nonprint media.

When broad-brush assessment tools, such as nationally normed, state-mandated standardized achievement tests, are privileged over other forms of assessment, the important perspectives of families, teachers, and students are silenced. Under these circumstances, assessment becomes something done *to* students and schools rather than a shared conversation *with* schools and their local communities. When assessment is done to schools, an adversarial relationship develops in which teachers and school administrators focus on how to raise test scores at the expense of learning. When broad-brush assessment tools are paired with punitive consequences in an effort to hold schools accountable for high standards, assessment conversations evolve into an "us versus them" contest in which the learners are the losers.

A common reaction to this feeling is to reject the value and credibility of the assessment procedure. At the same time, there is a breakdown in the relationship between those controlling the assessment and those who feel controlled by it. By contrast, the more ownership the various participants feel in the assessment process, the more seriously they value their own and others' stake in the process and the greater the possibility of quality assessment.

New technologies require changes in the ways we define literacy, and they offer new opportunities for assessing and reporting information about student learning. Electronic portfolios, data warehousing, Web-based assessment tools, and other digital innovations should prompt thoughtful conversations among all stakeholders to ensure that assessment information continues to inform instruction and to reflect the values of the local community, the needs of students and teachers, and the needs of the larger society.

11. Families must be involved as active, essential participants in the assessment process.

In many schools, families stand on the periphery of the school community, some feeling hopeless, helpless, and unwanted. However, the more families understand their children's progress in school, the more they can contribute to that progress. If teachers are to understand how best to assist children from cultures that are different from their own, families are a particularly important resource. Families must become, and be helped to become, active participants in the assessment process.

Public education today is characterized by unequal funding resources among school districts and by unequal participation of families in all aspects of school activities. The first characteristic is chiefly responsible for the unevenness among school districts in facilities, resources, quality teaching, sound learning, and healthy environments conducive to effective teaching and learning. The second condition contributes significantly to the difference between productive and unproductive schools. Arguably, the most effective schools have highly active participation by families in all aspects of governance and activities. Economic conditions and family participation are closely linked, however.

Family involvement in assessment, which is inseparable from curriculum, instruction, and learning, includes the following:

- Parents and other caregivers should be knowledgeable about assessment. Because of their own schooling backgrounds, many families believe that report-card grades and test results from multiple-choice examinations are the most productive and informative measures of their children's performance, knowledge base, and achievement. They need to become knowledgeable about the diverse possibilities for assessment, what those possibilities have to offer for understanding and assisting their child's development, and the uses and misuses of various forms of assessment.

- Families should be active participants in the assessment process and all other aspects of governance in their school community.

- Families have valuable knowledge of their children's development and situations that can contribute to the assessment process. Sharing this knowledge should be important and encouraged within all school communities.

- Families should seek ways to become more knowledgeable about their children's development.

Paying taxes alone does not constitute family participation in children's education. Teachers need the knowledge families have of their children, and school communities need the diversity of perspective that families bring to school problem solving, including assessment. Both families and schools are responsible for family involvement. Families must seek ways to become involved, and schools must organize to include families in their assessment and staff-development programs and actively seek their participation. This is particularly important in the case of families who are frequently marginalized by society in general and by the school system in particular. Newcomer families may need additional support to help them build an understanding of school culture and expectations and to enable them to access financial and social services.

Involving families in the assessment process includes involving them in staff development or community learning projects in which they learn more about reading and writing. It also includes the use of communication and reporting procedures between school and home that enable families to talk in productive ways with their children about their reading and writing. Involving families in the development of new reporting procedures is essential, since they are the primary audience for such reports.

The size and nature of the school community will have an impact on the ease with which families can be involved in schools and on the resources necessary to increase their participation. Consequently, this standard implies adequate and equitable funding of schools.

Case Studies

National Monitoring of Education

One important function of assessment is to monitor national changes in the education of young people so that the various stakeholders, including educators and the public and their representatives, can take any necessary actions to improve the quality of education. The following case studies present two examples, the National Assessment of Educational Progress (NAEP) in the United States and the National Educational Monitoring Project (NEMP) in New Zealand. Following the descriptions of these two national assessments, Table 1 on page 36 compares the ways in which they meet (or do not meet) the assessment standards.

Case 1: The United States' National Assessment of Educational Progress

The NAEP was developed as a test broad enough to cover what the designers considered appropriate educational domains including mathematics, reading, science, writing, the arts, civics, economics, geography, and U.S. history. The test, which was far too big for individual students to take, was then broken into smaller overlapping tests. These have been administered to a representative national sample of 9-, 13-, and 17-year-old students every four years since 1969. The four-year cycle was considered appropriate because shorter term systemic change was viewed as relatively unlikely.

The tests, which include multiple-choice and extended-answer questions, are administered by individuals hired and trained specifically for the purpose. The sampling system was designed to be nationally representative but is deliberately structured in such a way that comparisons cannot be made among states, school districts, or cities. Such comparisons were viewed as likely to increase the stakes involved and thereby encourage people to engage in activities such as "teaching to the test," which would then affect the extent to which the results could provide a valid representation of general achievement.

The NAEP results are presented to the public as scaled scores (from 0–300 or 0–500, depending on the subject) and at five percentiles through National Report Cards. Gains and (particularly) losses in performance are attended to by the press and politicians. The numbers remain relatively abstract since only a small percentage of the items are released for scrutiny by the public. The item structure of this long-term trend assessment test has been consistent since 1971 so that direct comparisons can be made over time. Participation is mandatory and sampling includes public and private schools, though in 2004 the private school sample was too small to be reported.

In 1990, politicians decided that enabling state-by-state comparisons would be a good idea, and energy was diverted to development of a second NAEP test. This second test, now called the "main NAEP," is administered at grades 4, 8, and 12, only in public schools. It allows state-by-state comparisons and, on a trial basis, comparisons of large urban districts. It is administered every two years and changes about every ten years to reflect curriculum changes. Tests are administered in science, math, reading, and writing. They are all administered in English. Some students are excluded for various reasons. Although participation in the state-level test had been voluntary, the No Child Left Behind Act of 2001 required states receiving Title I money to participate in the reading and math tests. Test items include multiple-choice, extended-answer, and short-answer questions, and results are reported both in scaled score performance levels and in categories of achievement (basic, proficient, and advanced) determined by cut scores. These are reported to the public by the press, though it seems likely that most who receive the information have little idea of what is meant by either the scaled scores or the categories (i.e., what it means to be "proficient").

Case 2: New Zealand's National Educational Monitoring Project

NEMP uses a national sampling of students over four-year cycles to assess 15 different areas of the national curriculum: art, music, speaking, listening, viewing, health and physical education, science, reading, writing, math, information skills, graphs, tables and maps, social studies, and technology. Knowledge, skills, motivation, and attitudes are all assessed. The assessment includes items addressing material not in the school curriculum in order to monitor the effects of any changes in the national curriculum. Students are assessed in English at two pivotal transition periods, year 4 (age 8–9) and year 8 (age 12–13). In Māori Medium settings, assessment is only at year 8. There is a deliberate effort to accommodate a range of differences in language, culture, gender, ability, and disability in the design and administration of assessment tasks. There are virtually no exclusions.

Almost all items are performance based, requiring students to work on tasks for three to four hours spread over five days, with the support of a trained teacher–test administrator. Tasks are selected to be meaningful and enjoyable for the students to ensure optimal engagement and the best picture of their capabilities. The task formats include working one-on-one with the teacher–administrator, working cooperatively in a group of four, and working independently on a series of hands-on activities or pencil-and-paper tasks. Some of the activities are videotaped and scored with rubrics. All items are carefully piloted.

In the NEMP, literacy is viewed as a social activity as much as a cognitive activity. For example, one task has a group of four year 4 students acting as the library committee. They are given a set of books and must choose, individually and then collectively, which books the library should purchase. The videotaped event is scored for the collaborative process as well as for individual performance.

School participation is voluntary; if a school is selected on multiple occasions or is unable to participate in a given testing, it is replaced with the most comparable school available. Replacement is rare because of a history of positive experiences. The test is administered by a group of teachers who are seconded from the schools, trained, and then returned to their teaching after the six-week test-administration period. Teachers are involved in the development of tasks, trialing of items, administration of tasks, and analysis of responses, and they report that the experience provides excellent professional development, which they share with their schools upon their return.

Results are reported to the public and to educators in terms of national performance and the performance of subgroups by demographics (e.g., race, gender, school size and characteristics). Results are reported in different formats to accommodate a wide audience, but typically they are reported in concrete terms of types of item citing specific examples. About two thirds of the items are released in order to maintain transparency and, in addition, so that teachers might use these items to see how their students compare with the national sample.

Table 1. Analysis of National Monitoring Cases 1 and 2 in Relation to the IRA–NCTE Assessment Standards

Assessment standard	Case 1: NAEP	Case 2: NEMP
1. The interests of the student are paramount in assessment.	Relatively little attention is paid to student interests in generating items. Although one aspect of the test invites a broad curriculum, increasing pressures associated with the test have curriculum-distorting potential.	Items are selected for student engagement. Assessments are closely tied to professional development in order to improve teaching. The assessment addresses a broad curriculum without high stakes that would distort the curriculum.
2. The teacher is the most important agent of assessment.	Little attention is paid to the teacher's role.	Teacher professional development is deliberately linked to training for test administration and scoring tasks.
3. The primary purpose of assessment is to improve teaching and learning.	There is no deliberate link between assessment and the improvement of teaching and learning, though, in recent years, there has been increasing pressure for higher generic scores.	Teacher professional development is specifically linked to training for administration and scoring tasks. Teachers are able to use excellent items as part of their instruction.
4. Assessment must reflect and allow for critical inquiry into curriculum and instruction.	The curriculum is addressed broadly in the lower stakes long-term test but less broadly in the higher stakes "main NAEP," increasing the likelihood of curriculum distortion in the latter test.	The curriculum is addressed broadly; communication of results is extensive and in plain language with concrete examples, and the performance of subgroups is analyzed. Because items go beyond the current curriculum, the effects of changes in curriculum can be analyzed.
5. Assessment must recognize and reflect the intellectually and socially complex nature of reading and writing and the important roles of school, home, and society in literacy development.	Items represent literacy as an individual cognitive activity with a modest degree of complexity relatively unconnected to home and society. The test recognizes the value to schools and society of a broad description of the consequences of education.	Items reflect the full complexity of literacy in a wide range of contexts and applications, both individual and social. Tasks are drawn from in-school and outside-school practices and deliberately attend to cultural and linguistic matters.

(continued)

Table 1. Analysis of National Monitoring Cases 1 and 2 in Relation to the IRA–NCTE Assessment Standards (continued)

Assessment standard	Case 1: NAEP	Case 2: NEMP
6. Assessment must be fair and equitable.	Items are selected and piloted to ensure fairness. Only one language is represented. Test performances are analyzed to reveal educational inequities. Private (mostly religious) schools are not clearly represented in the sampling system.	Items are selected and piloted to ensure fairness. Both primary cultural languages are represented. Item performances are analyzed to reveal educational inequities. If a school selected through the sampling system declines to participate, another school with similar characteristics is selected to ensure representation.
7. The consequences of an assessment procedure are the first and most important consideration in establishing the validity of the assessment.	The initial intention of an untainted indicator of national educational efforts is no longer realized because of changes in the sampling system (both items and students) that invite distorting pressures.	The consequence of the procedure is primarily professional development for teachers and a wide awareness of goals and progress in schooling. Because high stakes are not attached to the testing there is little incentive to distort the curriculum. These were central considerations in the design of the assessment.
8. The assessment process should involve multiple perspectives and sources of data.	The preparation of the test specifically includes a wide range of cultural and stakeholder representatives.	The preparation of the test specifically includes a wide range of cultural and stakeholder representatives.
9. Assessment must be based in the local school learning community, including active and essential participation of families and community members.	Local involvement is encouraged mostly through distribution of test results. Few items are released, which limits the meaningfulness of results to members of the public.	Local involvement is encouraged mostly through distribution of results and education of the public by providing extensive examples of test items and examples of the range of responses. This process regularly reminds the public of the breadth of the curriculum.

(continued)

Table 1. Analysis of National Monitoring Cases 1 and 2 in Relation to the IRA–NCTE Assessment Standards (continued)

Assessment standard	Case 1: NAEP	Case 2: NEMP
10. All stakeholders in the educational community—students, families, teachers, administrators, policymakers, and the public—must have an equal voice in the development, interpretation, and reporting of assessment information.	Representatives of various stakeholder groups are engaged in the development and trialing of the assessment items.	Representatives of various stakeholder groups are engaged in the development and trialing of the assessment items, an ongoing process since a large percentage of items is released to the public. Representatives are also convened to discuss and interpret the results as part of releasing information to the press. The assessment program is politically independent, limiting the relative power of some otherwise more powerful groups.
11. Families must be involved as active, essential participants in the assessment process.	Families have access to assessment information about changes in the effects of schooling.	Families have access to concrete, interpretable assessment information about changes in the effects of schooling.

School and Classroom Assessments: Response to Intervention in the United States

Beginning in 1975 in the United States, federal money was set aside for the education of children considered "handicapped." Children considered handicapped because of their failure to learn to read or write were classified as learning disabled because of a discrepancy between expected achievement (on the basis of a measure of intelligence) and actual achievement on an academic test.

Several problems arose with this process. First, the number of children classified as learning disabled expanded enormously. Second, a disproportionate number of minority students were so classified. Third, it took an extended period before the discrepancy was considered sufficient for these children to be classified and receive the benefit of the financial resources set aside for them. In the reauthorization of the federal Individuals With Disabilities Education Act (IDEA), an alternative was introduced to address these problems. Fifteen percent of the money allocated for special education could be used for intervention programs intended to prevent the need to classify children as learning disabled. The premise was that, before limited achievement could be assumed to be caused by a learning disability, instructional interventions should be attempted in order to rule out the possibility of inadequate instruction.

There are few actual requirements of the law. It requires that children's learning be monitored over time to determine whether instruction is effective ("data-based documentation of repeated assessments of achievement at reasonable intervals, reflecting formal assessment of student progress during instruction"). It requires that the instructional intervention is "scientific, research-based"—the definition of which is very broad. Finally, it requires that, in order to classify a child as learning disabled, there must be procedures and a committee (including the child's parents), a relevant classroom teacher, and "at least one person qualified to conduct individual diagnostic examinations of children."

Researchers and school districts have approached this in different ways. One family of Response to Intervention (RTI) approaches focuses on the use of intervention to identify students with learning disabilities. The other family of approaches focuses centrally on preventing students from needing to be classified as learning disabled. Examples of each are represented in these cases following, and a comparative analysis of the two is presented in Table 2 on page 42.

Case 3: An Identification Focus

One approach to implementing RTI involves screening children for potential difficulties using the Dynamic Indicators of Basic Early Literacy (DIBELS) to select those who are at risk of failure in reading. These children are given additional instructional attention. To ensure that no children who might need assistance are missed, children's reading progress is monitored from the middle of first grade on by measuring once each week how many words each child can read accurately from grade-level passages in one minute. The passages are standardized and norm-referenced, and reliability is emphasized. In kindergarten and the first half of second grade, progress is monitored by a measure of how quickly children can break a word into separate sounds and give a name and a sound for a letter. Trained aides, special education teachers, and the school psychologists complete most of the assessments in order to limit the testing time required of the classroom teacher. Students are given a comprehensive standardized reading test at the end of each year. Students who do not improve their reading speed and accuracy sufficiently, or at an adequate rate, after eight weeks are given a small-group instructional program taught by a trained teacher aide. Students who still do not increase their speed and accuracy receive an intensified intervention with increased time in a smaller group, taught by the literacy specialist.

These interventions are referred to as tiers, classroom instruction being tier 1, and successive interventions as tiers 2 and 3.

The instructional intervention is based on a program shown in experimental studies to be effective at increasing children's ability to read words with greater speed and accuracy according to the federal What Works Clearinghouse website. The program is a standardized intervention package with a set sequence of materials and a scripted instructional format. Fifteen minutes are spent on phonics, word recognition, and spelling regular and irregular words; five minutes on building speed with letter names, letter sounds, and word family patterns; and ten minutes reading short passages (3 to 4 words to over 40 words) based on sounds and words previously taught. During the ten minutes, comprehension questions integrating literal and inferential thinking are asked and strategies for locating answers are taught. Teachers are monitored by the school psychologist to ensure that they are implementing the program with fidelity—that is, as scripted.

Before initiating a new tier of intervention, a committee—directed by the school psychologist and including a classroom teacher, a parent (or surrogate), the principal, and a special education teacher—meets to decide whether the next phase is appropriate, given the assessments. Parents are kept informed using the graphs and norms of reading speed and accuracy. Those students who do not benefit from these interventions are referred by the committee to special education for individual instruction (tier 4) and classified as learning disabled. Failure to benefit from a validated form of instruction is seen as evidence of a learning disability.

Case 4: A Prevention Focus

This approach to RTI also involves layers of instruction, screening, and monitoring. On entering kindergarten, children are screened for their knowledge of the alphabet, and those with limited knowledge are given extra instructional support from the start on the assumption that limited alphabet knowledge reflects a limited literate history. Progress is monitored with an agreed upon portfolio of indicators including dated pieces of writing; an alphabet record for recording cumulative knowledge of letters, sounds, and related words noticed during classroom learning and one-on-one conferences; records of children's reading processes (strategies and accuracy); book difficulty level data; and anecdotal records. Some of these data are replaced in first and second grade with rubrics for judging writing, including writing stemming from reading. Comprehension is assessed through book discussions (small group, large group, and individual).

These portfolios are examined in monthly collaborative grade-level meetings led by a literacy coach who has 20% of her time designated for such administrative work. The coach is part of the school's commitment to improving instructional quality to reduce the need for additional interventions. At the end of each quarter, children's learning is evaluated at grade-level meetings led by the literacy coach and the principal in terms of end-of-grade expectations. These meetings include instructional planning.

The core classroom program has differentiated small-group instruction with the classroom teacher providing additional support for the lowest group. The school has a highly trained literacy coach who works with teachers 60% of her or his time to improve tier 1 instruction. Tier 2 is a small-group intervention with group size, amount of time, and teacher expertise determined by the students' needs, but with the framework consistent with tiers 1 and 3. Each is focused on interactions that support meaning making and independence. Tier 3 is a 1:1 intervention with Reading Recovery in first grade or a 1:2 group or reading/writing conferences in upper grades. (According to research and the federal What Works Clearinghouse website, Reading Recovery is a program shown in experimental studies to be effective at increasing children's ability to comprehend and to read and spell more accurately and to reduce the number of children becoming learning disabled.) The small-group interventions are carried out by Reading Recovery teachers and by special education teachers trained in the approach, and the literacy coach spends 20% of her or his time teaching these interventions. Tier 4 includes, as part of the referral process, close examination of the teaching interactions in tier 3 by an expert coach with collaborative attempts to change instructional interactions of students who are not adequately accelerating their ability to handle more difficult texts.

At the beginning of first grade, those children in the bottom half of the class are assessed using the Observation Survey of Early Literacy Achievement, a standardized procedure that offers instructionally useful information regarding literacy concepts, knowledge, and processes. This assessment is used to allocate students to tier 2 or 3. The intervention teachers keep daily records of writing, word work, and reading processes, and classroom teachers continue to accumulate portfolios of children's writing and running records of their reading. There is a comprehensive assessment at the end of each grade.

Before initiating a new tier of intervention, a committee, directed by the principal and the literacy coach and including the classroom teacher and a parent (or surrogate), meets to examine progress and next steps. Parents are kept informed of progress using half-year reports for all students and monthly descriptive feedback by intervention teachers using, for example, writing and text-level examples.

Table 2. Analysis of School and Classroom Cases 3 and 4 in Relation to the IRA–NCTE Assessment Standards

Assessment standard	Case 3: Identification focus	Case 4: Prevention focus
1. The interests of the student are paramount in assessment.	Instructional adaptations serve accurate diagnosis of disability and assumes that the student's interests are best served by identifying genuine and permanent handicaps so that subsequent accommodations can be made.	Instructional adaptations prevent initial difficulties from becoming disabilities and assumes that the student's interests are best served by attributing lack of progress to instructional inadequacies, prompting constant efforts at instructional improvement.
2. The teacher is the most important agent of assessment.	Teacher role is minimized in assessments by having others gather assessment data. Teacher role in intervention-as-assessment is also restricted by enforcing program fidelity, minimizing teacher adaptation for a particular child.	The teacher gathers ongoing formative data and individually and collaboratively negotiates instructional strategies based on those data. Teacher expertise is central in noticing, collecting, and responding to data in instruction/ intervention. The emphasis on ongoing coaching recognizes this.
3. The primary purpose of assessment is to improve teaching and learning.	The focus of assessment is on reliably determining which students are not benefiting from instruction rather than on providing instructionally useful information. Data collected on teaching are not to improve instructional interactions but to ensure instruction is not influenced by individuals.	Data are collected by the teacher to ensure they inform instruction. Regular stock-taking meetings are to counter individual biases and problem-solve instruction for students not accelerating adequately. Data are gathered specifically at tier 4 on instructional interactions to improve teaching.
4. Assessment must reflect and allow for critical inquiry into curriculum and instruction.	Data on teaching only allow for standardizing instruction and pointing to students for whom instruction is not working. Data do not inform the nature of instructional improvement. Because the focus of assessment is narrow (speed and accuracy of word reading), the differential effects of the larger literacy curriculum cannot be examined.	Data are collected on both teaching and learning that allow inquiry into curriculum and instruction. Assessments address a wide array of literacy (word knowledge, writing, comprehension) as well as teaching interaction patterns, enabling critical inquiry into the curriculum and its effects.

(continued)

Table 2. Analysis of School and Classroom Cases 3 and 4 in Relation to the IRA–NCTE Assessment Standards (continued)

Assessment standard	Case 3: Identification focus	Case 4: Prevention focus
5. Assessment must recognize and reflect the intellectually and socially complex nature of reading and writing and the important roles of school, home, and society in literacy development.	This case does not recognize literacy as social or complex and involves parents in the process of classifying a student as learning disabled.	This case recognizes literacy learning as social and somewhat complex.
6. Assessment must be fair and equitable.	Fairness is approached as ensuring due process, equal treatment, and reliable data and for providing accommodations for those with handicaps.	Fairness is viewed as requiring optimal instruction for all, which might be different for each.
7. The consequences of an assessment procedure are the first and most important consideration in establishing the validity of the assessment.	Reliability is considered the foundation of validity. Validity is tied to a narrow view of literacy. A valid assessment is considered to be one that accurately identifies students who are, in fact, learning disabled and does not identify those who are not.	An assessment process is considered valid if it leads to optimal instruction and the prevention of learning disability.
8. The assessment process should involve multiple perspectives and sources of data.	Multiple perspectives may be represented at the committee meeting. However, since data are narrow, there is limited likelihood that different perspectives will be invoked.	Multiple perspectives can be represented at quarterly grade-level meetings and at committee meetings. A broad range of data are available to invite and address different perspectives.
9. Assessment must be based in the local school learning community, including active and essential participation of families and community members.	Assessment is based in the local school learning community with limited participation of families.	Assessment is based in the local school learning community with limited participation of families.

(continued)

Table 2. Analysis of School and Classroom Cases 3 and 4 in Relation to the IRA–NCTE Assessment Standards (continued)

Assessment standard	Case 3: Identification focus	Case 4: Prevention focus
10. All stakeholders in the educational community—students, families, teachers, administrators, policymakers, and the public—must have an equal voice in the development, interpretation, and reporting of assessment information.	This standard is not sustained within this part of the school assessment system.	This standard is not sustained within this part of the school assessment system.
11. Families must be involved as active, essential participants in the assessment process.	Families are primarily involved at critical junctures.	Families are primarily involved at critical junctures.

Glossary of Assessment Terminology

Changes in the field of reading and writing assessment have generated a variety of new terms as well as new uses for established terms. The purpose of this glossary is to specify meanings for terms that are used frequently in discussions of literacy assessment.

Accountability

This term has dominated educational reform for at least the past decade. In its best sense, it means shared responsibility for constantly improving educational practices and short- and long-term educational consequences such as student learning and the qualities of the society the students develop. Policymakers, researchers, administrators, families, community members, teachers, and students all share this responsibility. Often, however, accountability focuses on the short-term responsibilities of teachers and students, such that primarily teachers and students experience the consequences when there are changes in achievement as measured by high-stakes tests. When teachers and students are held accountable only for short-term consequences, such as what can be measured on a test, longer term goals, particularly those not easily measured on a test, tend to be neglected. When only a subset of the community feels responsibility for educational improvement, education will not be well served and burn-out is likely to occur. An analogous situation would be holding a doctor accountable for a child's physical and mental health when the child has no health insurance (and therefore does not seek regular medical care) and his family's eating, exercising, and interaction patterns are not under the doctor's control.

Aggregation

In assessment, aggregation is the process of collecting data for the purpose of making a more general statement. For example, it is common practice for school districts to add together all students' test scores to find the average performance of students in the district. This process strips away all of the differences among the various cultural groups, schools, and students within the district in order to make the general statement. Even an individual student's test score is a result of aggregating all the items to which the student responded on the test to make a general statement about a student's "ability." It is also common to "disaggregate" scores to see how subgroups performed within the larger group or to investigate the students' performance in various subareas of reading (e.g., word identification, vocabulary, comprehension).

There are powerful tensions around aggregation reflecting, on the one hand, the need to make general statements about students, teachers, and schools and, on the other, the problem of stripping away the particulars of individual performances and situations in the process. Not everyone agrees that it is reasonable to reduce students or schools to numbers—let alone the purposes for or the grounds on which that might be done. It is often argued that administrators need highly aggregated data to make programmatic and budgetary decisions. However, both in education and in industry, administrators make different decisions when facing aggregated data than they do when presented with data about individual people and situations. Decision making needs to consider a balance of both kinds of data.

Authentic Assessment

For assessment to be considered authentic, it must include tasks that are a good reflection of the real-world activities of interest. This term arose from the realization that widely employed assessment tools generally have been poor reflections of what literate people actually do when they read, write, and speak. The logic of authentic assessment suggests, for example, that merely identifying grammatical elements or proofreading for potential flaws does not yield an acceptable measure of writing ability. Writing assessment tasks should reflect the audiences and purposes expected in life outside of school, with the real challenges those conditions impose. Similarly, reading very short passages and answering a limited number of multiple-choice questions is not a good measure of what literate people normally do when they read. Authentic assessments of reading employ tasks that reflect real-world reading practices and challenges. The authenticity of an assessment is very much a matter of the extent to which the assessment task measures what it purports to measure—a matter of construct validity.

Criterion-Referenced Assessment

We assess for particular purposes. When we want to know what children know and can do in a given domain, particularly whether they perform at a defined level on a specific task, we choose criterion-referenced assessment. Items in a criterion-referenced assessment are chosen because they discriminate what a person (or group) knows and can do and who has and has not reached a criterion level of performance. They are not chosen because they discriminate among individuals in determining who is better than whom. An item that genuinely measures a particular skill would not be eliminated from an assessment because everyone got it right. For example, a driver's test intends to determine whether a person is knowledgeable and capable enough to be allowed on the road, not whether one driver is more accomplished than another.

To be criterion referenced, a test must clearly define the characteristics that go into acceptable performance. In literacy, criterion-referenced assessments commonly compare students' performance on a specific task against established benchmarks. These benchmarks or criteria can be expressed as numerical ranges that define levels of achievement. For example, an 80–85 score may mean strong performance among levels of achievement ranging from unsatisfactory to outstanding. Criterion-based assessment can also involve holistic scoring of writing, for example, where a score is based on a set of pre-established criteria.

Compare to *norm-referenced assessment*.

Curriculum

We can think of curriculum as having three components: (1) the envisioned curriculum, (2) the enacted curriculum, and (3) the experienced curriculum. The envisioned curriculum is the intended proficiency of students as a consequence of instruction and participation in classroom events. The enacted curriculum is the daily attempt in classrooms to put the envisioned curriculum into practice. The experienced curriculum is the sense the learner makes of the enacted curriculum in the classroom and, thus, is constructed within the language of that classroom. For example, it is possible to intend to teach a particular lesson (e.g., authors' perspective) but that students not learn the lesson—either because it is not taught well (e.g., insufficient modeling, practice, support) or because the experiences of the students don't support the learning (e.g., they aren't provided with materials and experiences that invite perspective taking). As another example, if most of the reading material in one class includes racial or gender stereotypes, then that is likely to be reflected in students' learning. By contrast, students are likely to construct different knowledge about human relationships from a more balanced selection of reading material. However, the knowledge and attitudes students construct from those works are strongly influenced by the way teachers talk about them, the way teachers and other students respond to one another, and the nature of group discussions. Ultimately, it is the experienced curriculum that is our concern, and that is why students must be our primary curricular informants. However, the discrepancies among envisioned, enacted, and experienced curricula are what drive curriculum inquiry and the process of assessment.

Curriculum-Based Measurement (CBM)

This form of measurement was developed to help teachers evaluate a student's rate of growth in learning to read. The original idea was to have assessments that were embedded in the curriculum so they not only took no time away from teaching and learning but also did not distract teachers from the larger instructional picture. Originating in special education, a CBM of oral reading measures the number of words a child can read accurately in a minute from a standardized text (though there are comparable measures in spelling and writing). CBM assumes that a proxy variable, reading speed and accuracy (often mistakenly referred to as oral reading fluency), is an effective estimate of the larger construct of reading achievement and that the use of such estimates positively directs instruction.

Because these assessments now use texts and word lists that are standardized and that are not part of the curriculum, the term *curriculum based* is no longer particularly applicable. Other assessments not normally subsumed under the category of curriculum based, such as running records of children's reading and evidence of student work collected for a portfolio, are more clearly curriculum based since they are taken while the children are working within the actual classroom curriculum.

Equity

Issues of fairness surround literacy assessment. Testing originated as a means to control nepotism in job selection, providing an independent perspective on selection to uphold fairness. But equity cannot be assured through testing alone. Those who control the assessment process control what counts, what is valued. As we point out in this book's Introduction, language and literacy assessment is laden with cultural issues and biases. Although equity cannot be assured through assessment, it must be pursued relentlessly in assessment and in schooling. It is more likely to be achieved through the involvement of multiple, independent perspectives than through the use of a single perspective.

Tests have traditionally been administered, their results published, and their impact on instruction instigated with little regard to issues such as cultural, economic, or gender equity. But many equity issues affect assessment, rendering comparisons difficult and often invalid. Because traditional tests frequently reflect narrow cultural values, students and schools with different backgrounds and concerns often have not been fairly assessed.

Being equitable requires ensuring comparable educational experiences for those facing similar assessments, particularly in certification or gate-keeping situations. Questions of access to sound instruction, appropriate materials, and enriching learning opportunities are critical. Educators have become increasingly aware of the connections between assessment results and levels of safety, health, and welfare support in addition to physical accessibility.

Formative Assessment

Formative assessment, often referred to as assessment *for* learning, is the assessment that is done before and during teaching to inform instruction. It is assessment that informs instruction. Formative assessment includes things like teacher–student conferences, listening in on student book discussions, taking records of children's oral reading, examining students' writing pieces, and so forth. Though these assessments might be standardized, they often are not. To be formative, an assessment must affect instruction.

Compare to *summative assessment*.

High-Stakes Testing

These tests have significant consequences for those viewed as responsible for performance on the tests, and also for the student. For example, tests that determine whether one is accepted or rejected into the military, a university, or an educational program have significant consequences for the individual test takers. Consequences can be felt among a broader range of people, however. In the United States today, student test scores are not only used to determine whether children move on to the next grade level, but they also influence where educational resources are allocated and whether a school may continue to operate. Often, local news media publish school test scores, and property values are affected when families make decisions about where to purchase a home based on the local school's performance. When major consequences—such as the adjustment of teachers' salaries—are attached to their students' test scores, teachers will emphasize in their instruction what the test measures and reduce their emphasis on areas not covered by the test. This has consequences for the breadth of the curriculum and, thus, for the students' lives.

Both the National Council of Teachers of English and the International Reading Association have position statements regarding high-stakes testing. Both organizations recommend minimizing the stakes where possible and not relying on single measures, particularly when the stakes are high.

Inquiry

The process of inquiry begins with a genuine question, that is, a question that motivates the questioner to persist in seeking the answers. Authentic questions are rarely well formulated or structured at the outset. Rather, structure emerges through the process of inquiry. Inquiry is not merely a matter of asking and answering questions. It is a way of engaging the world and other people. Communication and social relationships play an important role in inquiry as questioners seek the advice and expertise of peers and more knowledgeable others, share their findings, reflect upon the results of the inquiry, and take up new questions that arise.

In a traditional view of classroom learning, teachers deliver information. They ask the children questions to which they already know the answers, and the students are to show they know the correct answers as well. This approach has not been very successful at helping all students become the critical, creative, and socially responsible citizens our society needs. In an inquiry classroom, on the other hand, students and teachers have a different relationship. Teacher and peers are resources for helping students answer their own questions. The community relationships are different. Instruction is based on engaging in sustained examination of personally significant topics.

Assessment as inquiry involves the same principles. It requires teachers to pose questions about the teaching and learning in their classrooms and to seek answers to those questions using assessment data and the resources of their learning community.

Multimodal Literacy

For centuries, the book has been the central medium of communication, expressed on paper largely through the mode of writing. Today, the screen is becoming the dominant medium of communication, with increasing reliance on the mode of image. A mode is a resource for communication and representation. Examples include speech, dance, gesture, music, sculpture, photography, and writing. Humans may express themselves through a single mode, such as writing, but with growing frequency we combine modes to communicate. This results in multimodal texts such as a PowerPoint presentation or YouTube video that combines words, images, music, and movement, or an advertisement in which print and image are merged. Today's and tomorrow's learners need to acquire competence in this multimodal literacy.

Norm-Referenced Assessment

When we want to know how a child performs relative to other children in a particular domain, we use norm-referenced assessment. Items in a norm-referenced assessment are chosen because they discriminate between individuals rather than assessing what a person (or group) knows and can do. To make norm-referenced assessments, assessment practices need to be standardized and test item selection must focus on maximizing the differences among individuals on a scale. An item that genuinely measured a particular skill but which all students got correct would not be used because it would not discriminate who was better than whom.

Norm-referenced interpretations are based on comparisons with others, usually resulting in a ranking. For example, a norm-referenced interpretation of a student's writing might assert that the sample is "as good as that of 20% of the students in that grade nationally."

Norm-referenced testing is the most prevalent form of large-scale testing, in which large groups of students take a test and the scores are grouped and interpreted in relation to other scores. In other words, the score of any student or group (school, district, state, or nation) has meaning only in relation to all the other scores of like entities (e.g., school to school, district to district, state to state). In order to make such comparisons, we have to make the assumption of "all else being equal," which is rarely justifiable. National norm-referenced tests assume that all students in our society have had similar cultural and curricular experiences. Uses of these tests also commonly ignore differences in curriculum, culture, gender, ethnicity, economic circumstance, per-pupil funding, and so forth.

The main advantage of such assessments is the simplicity of the linear scale. The seductiveness of this scale is also the main disadvantage, because the scores appear readily interpretable and objective. However, the score oversimplifies the complexities of literacy and assessment. Unfortunately, norm-referenced test scores often become the most important criterion for decisions about placement and promotion, which have a powerful impact on students' and teachers' lives.

Compare to *criterion-referenced assessment*.

Performance-Based Assessment

Performance-based assessment refers to assessment that involves the demonstration of a particular skill and often the process of accomplishing a performance specific to that skill. Performance assessments can include, for example, such complex activities as group collaboration to write and produce a play. The concept of performance-based assessment is related to the concept of authentic assessment in that it arose from a realization of the limitations of multiple-choice tests, and other assessments of complex skills, and the difficulty in making inferences about complex skills from such assessments.

Portfolio Assessment

A portfolio approach to assessment uses a systematic and multifaceted collection of work that represents a student's development. For example, a portfolio might include a range of writing pieces, a book log, self-reflections, group projects, and multimedia work. Because of the nature of the contents, portfolios are both curriculum based and performance based. A primary emphasis in most portfolio assessment is on student involvement and the development of self-assessment or reflectiveness. However, in some applications, portfolios can also include teacher and parent observations.

Reliability

Broadly speaking, reliability is an index of the extent to which a set of results or interpretations can be generalized over time, across tasks, and among interpreters. In other words, it is a particular kind of generalizability. For example, a common concern raised by newer forms of literacy assessment is whether different examiners, evaluating a complex response and using complex scoring criteria, will draw similar conclusions about a student's performance (whether an assessment will generalize across different examiners). Experience from scoring complex student writing samples suggests that high rates of agreement can be achieved when people are well trained in the application of specific criteria.

Another example of reliability is whether a score obtained by a student on a test would remain the same if the student took the test the following day, assuming no new learning has taken place—in other words, whether the performance generalizes over time. In general, the more samples of student work we collect, the more reliable and consistent an assessment will be.

Reliability is only important within the context of validity—the extent to which the assessment measures what it is supposed to measure and leads to useful, meaningful conclusions and consequences. Reliability does not guarantee a high-quality assessment. It is possible that consistent scoring can be achieved on poorly designed tests or tests of trivial skills. Indeed, reliability is easiest to obtain on low-level skills.

Summative Assessment

Summative assessment, often referred to as assessment *of* learning, is the after-the-fact assessment in which we look back at what students have learned, such as end-of-course or end-of-year examinations. The most familiar forms are the end-of-year standardized tests, though in classrooms we also assess students' learning at the end of a unit. These assessments are likely to be uniform or standardized.

Compare to *formative assessment*.

Validity

Historically, a common definition of a valid measure is that it measures the construct it purports to measure. This is called *construct validity*. For example, if we claim that an assessment measures reading fluency, but it only measures speed and accuracy and does not include aspects such as intonation, the test would have poor construct validity.

More recent conceptions of validity include an examination of the consequences of assessment practices—*consequential validity*. For instance, a test might have excellent construct validity as a measure of decoding ability. However, if it were used as the basis for adjusting teachers' salaries, resulting in an overemphasis on decoding in the curriculum, it would not be a valid assessment process. In other words, one cannot have a valid assessment procedure that has negative or misguided consequences for children. Consequently, a productive definition of a valid assessment practice would be one that reflects and supports the valued curriculum.